From Seeds to Plants

By Kaneisha Lhasa

Illustrated by Keiko Motoyama

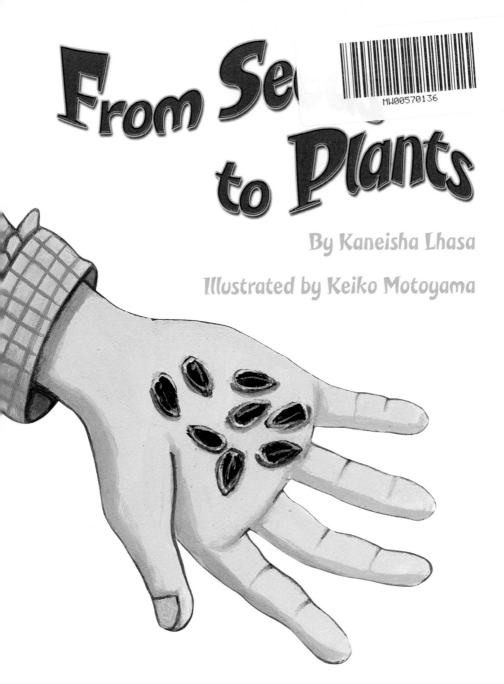

Target Skill Draw Conclusions

Grant can plant lots of seeds.

Can you see the seeds?

The seeds can get big.

That is what seeds can do!

Grant can see the big plant.

Can you see the tomatoes?

Meg can plant lots of seeds.
Can you see the seeds
in her hand?

The seeds can get big.

That is what seeds can do!

Meg can see the big plant.

Can you see the sunflowers?

Grant and Meg plant,
plant, plant!
What can they plant next?